Emily Post's Wedding Planner

by Elizabeth L. Post

a keepsake of the wedding of

_____

and

_____

on

_____

at

_____

FIRST EDITION

Designer: C. Linda Dingler

Library of Congress Cataloging in Publication Data

Post, Elizabeth L.
  Emily Post's Wedding planner.
    1. Wedding etiquette. I. Post, Emily, 1873–1960.
II. Title. III. Title: Wedding planner
BJ2051.P57   1982   395'.22   81-48168
ISBN 0-06-090935-8 (pbk.)   AACR2

395
P

82 83 84 85 86 10 9 8 7 6 5 4 3 2 1

Dear Bride and Groom:

The most important day of your life is rushing toward you. As it approaches, more and more decisions must be made and preparations started. This planner is designed to help the two of you make decisions, plan, and prepare for your wedding and reception. By organizing your thoughts and providing you with a means of keeping your arrangements indexed and clear, this planner will help you to relax and to enjoy these wonderful weeks. In the midst of all the excitement remember it's important for both of you to take time away from your preparations to spend with each other.

This planner is a book for the bride's mother, too. She will undoubtedly want to be involved in your wedding plans, and the records you keep here will be invaluable as she organizes *her* responsibilities. But always remember that it is your wedding and the final decisions are yours. Both of you may want to consult your parents to take full advantage of their interest and experience, but your parents *had* their wedding day—this one belongs to the two of you.

I wish you both the very best of luck, and that greatest blessing of all—a happy marriage.

Sincerely,

Elizabeth L. Post

*A*s your wedding draws closer you may find yourself lost in a swirl of planning and activities. At various times you may need to consult with members of your families or your bridal party. Use these pages to list everyone: both sets of parents; your brothers and sisters; all the members of your bridal party; and other friends or relatives you'll need to be in touch with. Be sure to list both home and business phone numbers since you never know when you might need to reach someone during the day.

Name	*Address*	*Telephone*

Name	Address	Telephone

Name	Address	Telephone

Name	Address	Telephone

Ready Reference for Important Names and Addresses

Farther along in this planner you'll find pages to help you decide which professionals will help make your wedding a truly memorable occasion. After you've chosen your special caterer, florist, photographer, and musician, transfer their names and addresses below to keep this information always at your fingertips. Remember to obtain the name of the person at each establishment who'll be handling your wedding so that you'll be sure and keep in touch with this person.

Reception site

    Name:
    Address:
    Telephone:

    Manager:

Caterer

    Name:
    Address:
    Telephone:

    Banquet manager:

Florist

>Name:
>Address:
>Telephone:
>
>Person to contact:

Photographer

>Name of studio:
>Address:
>Telephone:
>
>Photographer assigned to your wedding:
>
>Time photographer is to arrive at the wedding:

Musician

>Name of band:
>Agent's name:
>Address:
>Telephone:
>
>Person to contact:

Bride's Check-List

There are so many details that must be remembered if your wedding is to run smoothly that it is essential to have a very complete check-list at your fingertips. Your timetable should start three months before the wedding. It should be kept in a convenient place where it can be consulted regularly, and additions made or items crossed off as they are attended to. You may make a larger, more detailed timetable following the list below, if you wish, or you may check off the items here in this planner.

Three Months Ahead of the Wedding

1. Decide on the type of wedding and reception you want and the degree of formality and the size.
2. With your clergyman's cooperation, set the date and hour of the wedding.
3. With your fiancé, make an appointment for a personal talk with your clergyman.
4. Choose attendants and ask them to serve.
5. Make out your guest list and ask the groom and his family to send their lists to you as soon as possible. Tell them approximately how many guests they may invite, to stay within your limit. A card file is the most efficient system.
6. Order the invitations and announcements.
7. Order your bridal gown and those of your attendants.
8. Talk to the pastor, sexton, and organist about music, decorations, and procedure at the ceremony.
9. Engage the caterer if the reception is to be at home.
10. Reserve the club, hotel room, restaurant, or hall if the reception is not to be at home.
11. Engage the services of a florist.
12. Make an appointment with a photographer for your formal wedding portraits, and reserve time for candid shots the day of the wedding.

13. If you plan to have live music at your reception, hire the orchestra or musician.
14. Hire limousines, if necessary, for transporting the bridal party to the church and from the church to the reception.
15. If the wedding is to be at home, make arrangements for repairs, painting, cleaning.
16. If you wish, order notepaper for thank-you notes monogrammed with initials of your maiden name, and paper with your married initials for later.
17. Start to shop for your household trousseau and your personal trousseau.
18. Select your china, crystal, and silver patterns.

Two Months Before the Wedding

1. Notify your bridesmaids about their fittings and accessories. If possible, have shoes dyed in one lot.
2. Select gifts for your bridesmaids and a gift for your groom if you intend to give him one.
3. Go to local gift and department stores and list your choices in their bridal registries.
4. At the time of, or soon after, the final fitting of your wedding dress, have the formal bridal photographs taken.
5. Make detailed plans with the caterer or manager of your club or hotel. This includes menu, seating arrangements, parking, and so on.
6. Make medical and dental appointments, and be sure to make an appointment with your hairdresser for the day of your wedding or a day or two before.
7. Go apartment- or house-hunting with your groom.
8. Address and stuff wedding invitations when they arrive or obtain

envelopes when ordering invitations and address them earlier.

9. Make housing arrangements for out-of-town attendants and guests.

The Last Month

1. Mail the invitations three to four weeks before the wedding.
2. Check with your groom about his blood test and the marriage license.
3. With your groom, select your wedding ring—and his, if it is to be a double-ring ceremony.
4. Set up the tables for the display of wedding gifts.
5. Record all gifts and write thank-yous as they arrive.
6. Make a list of your honeymoon clothing and start setting it aside and packing as much as possible.
7. Check on all accessories for your wedding costume and also for those of your bridesmaids.
8. Make final arrangements with the professionals who are working with you—florist, photographer, caterer.
9. Change your name and address on all documents, such as driver's license and checking account.
10. Check your luggage to be sure it is adequate and in good condition.
11. See about a floater insurance policy to cover your wedding gifts—especially if you display them.
12. Arrange for a bridesmaids' luncheon if you wish to give one.
13. Address the announcements, enclose them in their envelopes, and give them to your mother or a friend to mail the day after the wedding.
14. Make arrangements for a place for the bridesmaids to dress. It is best if they are all together, whether in your home, at a friend's house, or in a room in the church.
15. Plan the seating of the bridal table and the parents' table at the reception, and make out place cards for them.
16. Send your wedding announcement to the newspapers, with your wedding portrait if you wish. Large papers will send you their own form to be filled out.

The Day of the Wedding

1. In the morning:
   Have hair done or shampoo and set it yourself.
   Pick up any orders that are not to be delivered—flowers, food, etc.
2. Two hours before ceremony:
   Have bridesmaids arrive at your home to dress and to assist you with last-minute chores or emergencies.
3. One hour before:
   Bathe and dress.
   Ushers should arrive at church at least forty-five minutes before ceremony to plan duties and **seat** early arrivals.
   If you and your attendants are dressing at the church or synagogue, you should arrive now.
4. One half hour before:
   Groom and best man arrive at church.
   Background music starts.
   First guests arrive and are seated.
   If you have dressed at home you and attendants go to church and wait in private room or corner of vestibule.
   Best man, on arrival, checks last-minute arrangements with clergyman and gives him his fee.
5. Fifteen minutes before:
   Family members and honored guests (godparents, for example) arrive and are seated "behind the ribbon" or in the pews near the front.
   The carpet is rolled down the aisle.
6. Five minutes before:
   The groom's mother and father arrive, and she is escorted in, followed by her husband (unless he is the best man). Finally, just before the music starts for the processional, the bride's mother is escorted to her seat in the front row, her husband takes his place beside the bride, and the pew ribbons are put in place.
   The attendants take their places in the proper order for the processional.
7. At precisely the time stated on the invitation, the music starts and the ushers lead the procession down the aisle.

First Big Decisions

Before you get down to the smaller details, there are certain major decisions that must be made as soon as you start to plan your wedding. You must decide whether you wish to have a small or a large wedding, a formal or an informal wedding, and where you want it to take place. You will also want to select your attendants immediately. The following pages present various options and allow you space to make notes.

	Formal	Semiformal	Informal
Bride's dress	Long white gown, train, veil optional	Long white gown, veil optional	White or pastel cocktail dress or suit or afternoon dress (sometimes, very simple long gown)
Bridesmaids' dresses	Long or according to current style	Long or according to current style	Same type of dress as worn by bride
Dress of groom and his attendants	Cutaway or tailcoat	Sack coat or tuxedo	Dark blazer or jacket
Bride's attendants	Maid or matron of honor, 4–10 bridesmaids, flower girl, ring bearer (optional)	Maid or matron of honor, 2–6 bridesmaids, flower girl, ring bearer (optional)	Maid or matron of honor, 1 or 2 children (optional)
Groom's attendants	Best man; 1 usher for every 50 guests, or same number as bridesmaids	Best man; 1 usher for every 50 guests, or same number as bridesmaids	Best man; 1 usher if necessary to seat guests

	Formal	*Semiformal*	*Informal*
Location of ceremony	Church, synagogue, or large home or garden	Church, synagogue, chapel, hotel, club, home, garden	Chapel, rectory, justice of the peace, home, garden
Location of reception	Club, hotel, garden, or large home	Club, restaurant, hotel, garden, home	Church parlor, home, restaurant
Number of guests	200 or more	75 to 200	75 or under
Provider of service at reception	Caterer at home, or club or hotel facilities	Caterer at home, or club or hotel facilities	Caterer, friends and relatives, or restaurant
Food	Sit-down or semi-buffet (tables provided for bridal party, parents, and guests); hot meal served; wedding cake	Buffet (bridal party and parents may have tables); cocktail buffet food, sandwiches, cold cuts, snacks, wedding cake	Stand-up buffet or 1 table for all guests; may be a meal or snacks and wedding cake
Beverages	Champagne; whiskey and soft drinks (optional)	Champagne or punch for toasts; whiskey and soft drinks (optional)	Champagne or punch for toasts; tea, coffee, or soft drinks in addition

	Formal	*Semiformal*	*Informal*
Invitations and announcements	Engraved	Engraved	Handwritten or telephoned invitations; engraved announcements
Decorations and accessories	Elaborate flowers for church, canopy to church, aisle carpet, pew ribbons, limousines for bridal party, groom's cake (given to guests in boxes), engraved matchbooks or napkins as mementos, rose petals or confetti	Flowers for church, aisle carpet, pew ribbons, rose petals (other items optional)	Flowers for altar, rose petals
Music	Organ at church (choir or soloist optional); orchestra for dancing at reception	Organ at church (choir or soloist optional); strolling musician, small orchestra, or records for reception; dancing optional	Organ at church; records at reception optional

The Wedding Ceremony

One of your first decisions will be the site for your wedding. When you have made your final choice record all the pertinent information here.

Church: (Name)
    Address:
    Telephone:
    Clergyman's name and number:
    Organist's name and number:
    Sexton's name and number:

    Date and time of wedding ceremony:

If you wish to write your own vows or have special passages read during the ceremony be sure to discuss this with your clergyman. Keep track of those passages you'd like to include on page 59. Remember to bring these along when you meet with your clergyman. Also, note any special regulations or requirements you'll have to meet before the ceremony can take place.

    Appointments to see clergyman:
    1. Date: Time:
    2. Date: Time:

    Special regulations or requirements:

Be sure to make a reservation for the rehearsal at the time you make the reservation for your wedding ceremony. On page 54 you'll find room to list all those who should attend the rehearsal. Remember to notify the members of your bridal party about the day and time of the rehearsal. Make a check mark in the margin when you've done this.

    Date and time of rehearsal:

The Traditional Division of Expenses

The division of expenses listed below is the traditional one, and there are, of course, many variations. Today the groom's family often offers to pay a share. It is quite acceptable for the bride's parents to accept this offer, especially if the groom and his family would like a larger or more elaborate reception than the bride's parents can afford. Use these pages as a guide, and make your own adjustments.

Expenses of the Bride and Her Family

Services of a bridal consultant and/or a secretary

Engraved invitations and announcements (While true engraving is the most beautiful and appropriate for a formal wedding, fine simulated engraving is acceptable and saves considerable expense)

The bride's wedding dress and accessories

Floral decorations for church and reception, bridesmaids' flowers, bride's bouquet (in some areas, given by groom)

Formal wedding photographs and candid pictures

Music for church and reception

Transportation of bridal party to church, and from church to reception, if rented limousines are used

All expenses of reception, including rental of hall or club, catering service, food, refreshments (including liquor, if it is to be served), wedding cake, and favors

Bride's presents to her attendants

Bride's present to groom, if she wishes to give him one

The groom's wedding ring, if it is to be a double-ring ceremony

Rental of awning for church entrance and carpet for aisle, if not provided by church

Fee for services performed by sexton. His fee may include that for the organist or choir. If not, he will inform you of what that charge is.

A traffic policeman if necessary

Accommodations for bridesmaids if necessary

Expenses of the Groom and His Family

Bride's engagement and wedding rings

If he wishes, a present to his bride (usually jewelry)

Gifts for the best man and ushers

Hotel accommodations for his attendants, when necessary

Ties, gloves, and boutonnieres for the ushers, and his own bouton-
niere

The clergyman's fee or donation

The marriage license

Transportation for himself and his best man to the church

Expenses of the honeymoon

The rehearsal dinner (not obligatory, but becoming more and more
customary)

The bride's bouquet, in areas where local custom requires it

The bride's going-away corsage

Corsages for immediate members of both families (unless bride has
included them in her florist's order)

Bachelor dinner, if he wishes to give one

Groom's parents pay their own transportation and lodging expenses

Bridesmaids' Expenses

Purchase of bridesmaids' dresses and all accessories
Transportation to and from the city or town where the wedding takes place
A contribution to a gift from all the bridesmaids to the bride
An individual gift to the couple
A shower and/or luncheon for the bride

Ushers' Expenses

Rental of wedding attire
Transportation to and from location of wedding
A contribution to a gift from all the ushers to the groom
An individual gift to the couple
The bachelor dinner, if given by the ushers

Out-of-town Guests' Expenses

Guests who come from a distance pay their own travel and lodging expenses. The parents of the bride or groom should assist their relatives and friends by making reservations, and of course, may offer to pay any expenses they wish to assume.

Reservations Made For	Name and Address of Hotel or Motel	Telephone

Sample Budget

Semi-formal Wedding, 100 Guests, 4 Attendants, Reception Held in Club or Catered at Home

Wedding attire	$250
Invitations and announcements	250
Flowers for church and reception	150
Flowers for bridesmaids	150
Music for church	50
Music for reception	300
Limousines for bridal party (if necessary)	100
Photographs (formal and candid)	350
Bridesmaids' gifts	100
Reception expenses (food, drink, service)—$20 per person	2,000
Incidentals (sexton's fee, groom's ring, etc.)	200
	$3,900

Notes:

_____

_____

_____

_____

_____

_____

_____

_____

_____

Your Budget

Write down the amount you think you can spend on each item in the second column and the amount you actually spend in the third.

Item	*Projected Amount*	*Amount Spent*
Wedding attire		
Invitations and announcements		
Flowers for church and reception		
Flowers for bridesmaids		
Limousines (if necessary)		
Photographs		
Bridesmaids' gifts		

Reception expenses
  Food
  Beverages
  Favors
  Cake
  Music
  Incidentals		

Dress for Bridal Party and Guests

The clothing selected by the bridal party and guests is determined by the formality of the ceremony. Use this chart to guide you in your selections.

	Most Formal Daytime	*Most Formal Evening*	*Semiformal Daytime*
Bride	Long white dress, train, and veil; gloves optional	Same as most formal daytime	Long white dress; short veil and gloves optional
Bride's attendants	Long dresses, matching shoes; gloves are bride's option	Same as most formal daytime	Same as most formal daytime
Groom, his attendants, bride's father	Cutaway coat, striped trousers, pearl gray waistcoat, white stiff shirt, turndown collar with gray-and-black-striped four-in-hand or wing collar with ascot, gray gloves, black silk socks, black kid shoes	Black tailcoat and trousers, white piqué waistcoat, starched-bosom shirt, wing collar, white bow tie, white gloves, black silk socks, black patent-leather shoes or pumps or black kid smooth-toe shoes	Black or charcoal sack coat, dove gray waistcoat, white pleated shirt, starched turndown collar or soft white shirt with four-in-hand tie, gray gloves, black smooth-toe shoes
Mothers of couple	Long or short dresses; hat, veil, or hair ornament; gloves	Usually long evening or dinner dress, dressy short cocktail permissible; veil or hair ornament if long dress; small hat, if short; gloves	Long or street-length dresses, gloves; head covering optional
Women guests	Street-length cocktail or afternoon dresses (colors are preferable to black or white); gloves; head covering optional	Depending on local custom, long or short dresses; if long, veil or ornament—otherwise, hat optional; gloves	Short afternoon or cocktail dress; head covering for church optional
Men guests	Dark suits; conservative shirts and ties	If women wear long dresses, tuxedos; if short dresses, dark suits	Dark suits

	Semiformal Evening	Informal Daytime	Informal Evening
Bride	Same as semiformal daytime	Short afternoon dress, cocktail dress, or suit	Long dinner dress or short cocktail dress or suit
Bride's attendants	Same length and degree of formality as bride's dress	Same style as bride	Same style as bride
Groom, his attendants, bride's father	Winter, black tuxedo; summer, white jacket; pleated or piqué soft shirt, black cummerbund, black bow tie, no gloves, black patent-leather or kid shoes	Winter, dark suit; summer, dark trousers with white linen jacket or white trousers with navy or charcoal jacket; soft shirt, conservative four-in-hand tie; hot climate, white suit	Tuxedo if bride wears dinner dress; dark suit in winter, lighter suit in summer
Mothers of couple	Same as semiformal daytime	Short afternoon or cocktail dresses	Same length dress as bride
Women guests	Cocktail dresses, gloves; head covering for church optional	Afternoon dresses, gloves; head covering for church optional	Afternoon or cocktail dresses, gloves; head covering for church optional
Men guests	Dark suits	Dark suits; light trousers and dark blazers in summer	Dark suits
Groom's father:	He may wear the same costume as the groom and his attendants, especially if he is to stand in the receiving line. If he is not to take part, however, and does not wish to dress formally, he may wear the same clothes as the men guests.		

Clothes for Your Bridal Party

The experienced personnel in your department store or bridal shop will be best qualified to help you select your gown. It is not necessary to exceed your budget; shop around if you do not find something within your budget at once. Don't get carried away by a trendy style—the long white traditional gown is the most flattering costume a bride can wear.

When you select your bridesmaids' dresses, consider their finances. Try to choose dresses that can be worn afterwards with simple alterations.

Bride's Attire
   Store:
   Address: Telephone:
   Description (color, material, style, etc.):

   Salesperson:
   Date ordered:
   Fitting appointments:

To ensure a perfect fit, be sure to wear the undergarments and shoes you'll wear for the wedding when you go for your fittings.
   Pick-up time:

Accessories
   Shoes:
   Headdress:
   Jewelry:
   Other:

Notes

As soon as she selects her dress, the mother of the bride should let the mother of the groom know what style and color she has chosen. The mother of the groom can then pick out a complementary dress. Record their choices below.

Mother of the Bride
    Store:
    Address: Telephone:
    Description:
    Salesperson:
    Fitting appointment:
    Pick-up date:
    Accessories:

Mother of the Groom
    Store:
    Address: Telephone:
    Description:
    Salesperson:
    Fitting appointment:
    Pick-up date:
    Accessories:

Fathers of the Bride and Groom

Since he will escort his daughter down the aisle, the father of the bride will wear the same style clothing as the groom and his attendants. The father of the groom may wear the same clothing as his son and his son's attendants, and should do so if he will stand in the receiving line.

Attendants' Dresses
Store:
Address: Telephone:
Description:
Salesperson:

Accessories:

Ordered on:
Will be ready for fittings by:
Delivery date:

SIZES

Attendant's Name	Dress	Shoe

If possible, get samples of dress material to help in selecting flowers and having shoes dyed.

Attendants who live nearby should make their own appointments for fittings. Dresses should be mailed to others in time for them to have any necessary alterations made. If you've decided to have a flower girl in your bridal party be sure to include her here, and don't forget to inform her parents when her dress will be ready too.

Groom and Ushers

The groom, his best man, and the ushers will wear identical outfits, except that the groom may select an ascot or tie in a different pattern. The clothes are almost always rented, and should be ordered from the same rental agency so that they will match. Ask out-of-town ushers to send their sizes and measurements well in advance so that the groom can reserve their outfits for them.

Store:
Address: Telephone:
Description

Salesperson:

Ordered on: Ushers may go in for fittings on:
Pick-up and return times:

| | SIZES | | | | | |
Name	Regular Size	Waist	Trouser Length	Collar	Sleeve Length	Shoe

If you're having a ring bearer in your bridal party include him here and don't forget to inform his parents when his clothing will be ready too.

Selecting Your Caterer, Florist, Musicians and Photographer

Unless you have a favorite in any of these categories already selected, you will want to shop around to be sure you are getting the best service for the best price. Use the following pages to make notes of what services each establishment offers and what the cost would be.

Here are some questions you might want to ask when selecting a caterer:

Does this caterer offer a wedding package?

If so, what does it contain and what does it cost?

Are substitutions permissible?

What food and drinks will be served at the cocktail hour? the reception? Will brand name liquors be served? Will there be an open bar for the cocktail hour and reception? either? both?

What does a sample place setting consist of? Can you sample the food and observe a party arranged by this caterer? Will the caterer provide printed directions to the catering hall for you to include with your invitations? Is insurance against china and crystal breakage included in the costs stated? If not, is it available and at what cost?

At what time do the servers go on overtime pay? Does the caterer offer the option of extending the reception an extra hour? at what cost?

Be sure to have all these details spelled out before signing a contract with your chosen caterer.

Once you've decided on a caterer discuss whether you'd prefer to have the caterer or your own baker provide the wedding cake. Ask both the caterer and your baker for a sample of the wedding cake to make sure it's to your liking. Also, remember to tell your caterer about any details that are special to your wedding. For instance, if you are inviting out-of-town guests who you know enjoy certain regional specialty refreshments inform the caterer of any special ingredients these might call for. Your guests will appreciate your thoughtfulness.

Caterer

Name:
Address: Telephone:
Menus available:

Type of service (sit-down, buffet, etc.):

Help provided (waiters, bartenders, parking valet, etc.):

Wedding cake:

Tables and chairs:

Other services and equipment:

Price per person:
Additional costs:
Gratuities:
Estimated total:

Caterer

Name:
Address: Telephone:
Menus available:

Type of service (sit-down, buffet, etc.):

Help provided (waiters, bartenders, parking valet, etc.):

Wedding cake:

Tables and chairs:

Other services and equipment:

Price per person:
Additional costs:
Gratuities:
Estimated total:

Caterer

   Name:
   Address: Telephone:
   Menus available:

Type of service (sit-down, buffet, etc.):

Help provided (waiters, bartenders, parking valet, etc.):

Wedding cake:

Tables and chairs:

Other services and equipment:

   Price per person:
   Additional costs:
   Gratuities:
   Estimated total:

The Florist

Flowers add a lovely touch of color to any wedding. You'll want to make an appointment to speak with several florists to find one who'll add that perfect finishing touch of color to your wedding. Remember not to limit yourself to looking at catalogs of floral arrangements, ask to see samples of each florist's work.

Among the questions you might want to ask a florist are:

Does this florist offer a wedding package? What does it consist of? Is it possible to substitute different types of flowers for those in the package, and what are the costs involved?

Perhaps you prefer silk flowers. Does this florist handle them? If you choose silk flowers you might consider having your bridal bouquet made into a table centerpiece for your home. Could this florist do this for you?

What are this florist's delivery charges? If flowers are to be delivered to more than one location, the bride's home, church, and reception site for instance, what effect does this have on delivery charges?

Name:
Address:
Telephone:
Flowers for church:
   Description:
   Price:
Flowers for reception:
   Description:
   Price:
Bridesmaids' flowers:
   Description:
   Price:
Bride's bouquet:
   Description:
   Price:
Boutonnieres:
   Description:
   Price:
Corsages for mothers:
   Description:
   Price:
Others:
   Description:
   Price:
Services (delivery, removal, other):
Estimated total:

Name: Name:
Address: Address:
Telephone: Telephone:
Flowers for church: Flowers for church:
  Description: Description:
  Price: Price:
Flowers for reception: Flowers for reception:
  Description: Description:
  Price: Price:
Bridesmaids' flowers: Bridesmaids' flowers:
  Description: Description:
  Price: Price:
Bride's bouquet: Bride's bouquet:
  Description: Description:
  Price: Price:
Boutonnieres: Boutonnieres:
  Description: Description:
  Price: Price:
Corsages for mothers: Corsages for mothers:
  Description: Description:
  Price: Price:
Others: Others:
  Description: Description:
  Price: Price:
Services (delivery, removal, other):   Services (delivery, removal, other):
Estimated total: Estimated total:

The Musicians

Shakespeare called music the food of love, and what an aura of romance the right music creates! When considering various orchestras remember to arrange to hear them play at a wedding or other social gathering rather than in a nightclub. You'll want to hear the different varieties of music the orchestra can provide for your wedding.

Name of orchestra:
Agent:
Address:

Telephone:

Number of pieces:
Instruments:

Length of playing time
and rest periods:

Requirements: (chairs, piano,
electrical needs, etc.)

Price:
Time and place to hear
the orchestra play:

Comments:

Name of orchestra:
Agent:
Address:

Telephone:

Number of pieces:
Instruments:

Length of playing time
and rest periods:

Requirements: (chairs, piano,
electrical needs, etc.)

Price:
Time and place to hear
the orchestra play:

Comments:

Name of orchestra:
Agent:
Address

Telephone:

Number of pieces:
Instruments:

Length of playing time
   and rest periods:

Requirements: (chairs, piano,
   electrical needs, etc.)

Price:
Time and place to hear
   the orchestra play:

Comments:

1. Strolling player
      Name:
      Agency:
      Address:
      Telephone:
   Instrument:
   Price per hour:

2. Strolling player
      Name:
      Agency:
      Address:
      Telephone:
   Instrument:
   Price per hour:

3. Strolling player
      Name:
      Agency:
      Address:
      Telephone:
   Instrument:
   Price per hour:

The Photographer

Visit several photo studios and study the quality of work each offers before deciding to whom you'll entrust the job of photographing your wedding. Be sure to study the samples of the photographer who'll actually photograph your wedding. Listed are some questions to help you compare photo packages, options, and prices before making your decision.

Name:
Address:
Telephone:

Does the photo studio offer a photo
    package?   _____

What does it consist of?
What does it cost for additions to the
package?   _____

What are the costs of

    Formal portraits of the bride: _____

    Formal portraits of bridal party: _____

What is the number of proofs taken at:
    The wedding?   _____

    The reception?   _____
What is the number of pages in the
    standard wedding album?   _____
    The cost?   _____

What does it cost per extra album page?   _____

What is the size and cost of extra albums?   _____

What is the cost of keeping all the proofs?   _____
Will the photographer stay through the
    entire reception? or just through the
    cutting of the cake?   _____

Name: Name:
Address: Address:
Telephone: Telephone:

_____   _____

_____   _____

_____   _____

_____   _____

_____   _____

_____   _____

_____   _____

_____   _____

_____   _____

_____   _____

_____   _____

Invitations, Announcements and Guest List

Your invitations will, in a way, set the tone of your wedding. If you are having an elegant formal wedding, your invitations should be elegant and formal, too. The most formal invitation is the traditional, engraved one, with the wording all in the third person. Many people object to the stiffness of that form and prefer a more personal wording, though beautifully printed or engraved. If engraving does not fit in your budget you can choose printing techniques that can hardly be distinguished from fine engraving but are much less expensive. The options are yours—consult your stationer and look at the samples. And remember that the simplest invitations, without frills and adornments, are in the best taste.

Stationers
Name:
Address and Telephone:
Estimate:
Design Chosen:
Quantity:

Name:
Address and Telephone:
Estimate:
Design Chosen:
Quantity:

Name:
Address and Telephone:
Estimate:
Design Chosen:
Quantity:

Place a check mark in the margin next to the stationer you've selected. Make a note of the day your order is to be ready.

In addition to your invitations and announcements, check with your stationer for favors you might wish to order for your reception. You might check whether the favors you want are available in one of the colors you've selected for your bridal party.

Matchbooks
    folding or box

with monogram and the date
    quantity and cost

with your names and the date
    quantity and cost

Cocktail Napkins
with a monogram and the date
    quantity and cost

with your names and the date
    quantity and cost

If you decide to order favors be sure to note when they'll be ready (if the date is different from the date your invitations and announcements will be ready).

Many wedding ceremonies and/or receptions end with the guests showering the bride and groom with a cascade of rice. A nice change of pace, especially for an outdoor wedding, is the use of birdseed for this purpose. Lovelier still is to order paper rose petals from your stationer. If you've decided to include one of these options in your wedding remember to order your choice ahead of time.

Use this page to decide on the exact wording of your wedding invitation. Make sure you take a copy with you when you visit stationers.

Date and time invitations are to be picked up:

Use this page to determine the wording of your wedding announcement, if you'll be sending announcements. The announcements should be ordered at the same time as the invitations.

Date and time announcements are to be picked up:

Guest List

This list provides a quick, at-a-glance reference. You can also keep an indexed file with each guest's name and address on an individual card.

Guest List

_____   _____

_____   _____

_____   _____

_____   _____

_____   _____

_____   _____

_____   _____

_____   _____

_____   _____

_____   _____

_____   _____

_____   _____

_____   _____

_____   _____

_____   _____

_____   _____

_____   _____

Guest List

_____   _____

_____   _____

_____   _____

_____   _____

_____   _____

_____   _____

_____   _____

_____   _____

_____   _____

_____   _____

_____   _____

_____   _____

_____   _____

_____   _____

_____   _____

_____   _____

Guest List

_____ _____

_____ _____

_____ _____

_____ _____

_____ _____

_____ _____

_____ _____

_____ _____

_____ _____

_____ _____

_____ _____

_____ _____

_____ _____

_____ _____

_____ _____

_____ _____

Guest List

_____   _____

_____   _____

_____   _____

_____   _____

_____   _____

_____   _____

_____   _____

_____   _____

_____   _____

_____   _____

_____   _____

_____   _____

_____   _____

_____   _____

_____   _____

_____   _____

Showers and Parties

In the midst of all the fun and excitement of planning your wedding, you will want to keep track of the wonderful showers and parties given in your honor. Use these pages to record the names and addresses of those friends and relatives who attended these parties. You can also use these lists to send thank-you notes to those you're unable to thank in person.

Type of shower:
  Hostess/Host:
  Date and time:
  Location: Telephone:

GUESTS

Name   *Address*

Type of shower:
  Hostess/Host:
  Date and time:
  Location: Telephone:

GUESTS

Name   *Address*

_____

_____

_____

_____

_____

_____

_____

_____

_____

_____

_____

_____

_____

_____

_____

_____

_____

_____

Other Parties Honoring the Bride and Groom

Kind of party (luncheon, cocktail, etc.):
Hostess/Host:
Place:
Date and time:

GUESTS

Name   *Address*

_____

_____

_____

_____

_____

_____

_____

_____

_____

_____

_____

_____

_____

_____

_____

_____

_____

_____

Kind of party (luncheon, cocktail, etc.):
Hostess/Host:
Place:
Date and time:

GUESTS

Name   *Address*

_____

_____

_____

_____

_____

_____

_____

_____

_____

_____

_____

_____

_____

_____

_____

_____

_____

_____

The Wedding Rehearsal

To be sure that everything goes smoothly during the wedding ceremony the rehearsal is vitally important. The two of you and your attendants should take the rehearsal seriously, arriving on time, properly dressed.

Many years ago the bride chose a stand-in for the rehearsal, since it was considered unlucky for her to actually say any of the words of the ceremony. Today however, both of you take your places at the altar, although the clergyman does not go through the whole service. He will however, let you rehearse your responses if you wish.

As well as practicing the processional and the recessional, and going through the service, the ushers should be briefed on who will sit in the reserved pews, and instructed on how the other pews should be filled. It should also be decided at this time which ushers will roll out the carpet and put the ribbons on the ends of the pews, who will escort the mothers, etc.

If special music is to be played, poems to be read, or nontraditional vows said, those should be practiced at the rehearsal so that they will be performed easily and naturally during the ceremony itself.

The groom's parents may be invited to attend, but their presence is not necessary since they have no active part in the ceremony. In order that they not feel left out, the two of you should extend an invitation to them but give them the option of not attending if that is what they wish. They may prefer to use that time in making the final preparations for the rehearsal dinner.

People Present at Rehearsal

List attendants and check off as they are notified of time, dress, and other details

Bride's attendants   Groom's attendants

_____   _____

_____   _____

_____   _____

_____   _____

_____   _____

_____   _____

_____   _____

Ring bearer: Flower girl:

Mother of the Bride:

Bride's escort:

Clergyman:

Organist:

Soloist:

Others:

Rehearsal Dinner

Although the groom's family usually gives the rehearsal dinner, you may be able to help by assisting with the guest list, and, if they come from out of town, by reserving a place and making many of the arrangements.

Name (club, hotel, restaurant):
Name of manager:
Address: Telephone:

Menu:

Beverages:

Music or entertainment:

Guests

_____   _____   _____

_____   _____   _____

_____   _____   _____

_____   _____   _____

_____   _____   _____

_____   _____   _____

_____   _____   _____

The Ceremony

Flowers for Church

Altar arrangements:	Ends of pews:
Description:	Description:
Price:	Price:
Others:	Others:
Description:	Description:
Price:	Price:

Notes:

Music for Ceremony

Organ selections preceding ceremony:_____

_____

_____

_____

Processional selection:_____

Recessional selection:_____

Soloist
  Name:
  Address and telephone:
  Selections:

Organist's fee:
Soloist's fee (if professional):

Suggested Selections:

Music for the ceremony should be joyous and meaningful, but "popular" music is not acceptable in many churches and synagogues. Traditional love songs—such as "I Love You Truly" or "Oh Promise Me" may be played in some churches, but not in others. The traditional wedding march is out of favor, but still means "Here Comes the Bride" to me. Your organist will help you choose music that is fitting and suits your taste.

Reserved Pews

Several pews in the front of the church may be reserved for relatives and close friends of the bride and groom. If you choose to send out reserved pew cards, those holding them should bring them to the church and show them to the usher escorting them. At a small wedding where the ushers know all the guests, cards are not always sent and the ushers are told which guests are to be seated "within the ribbons."

Bride's guests seated in reserved pews
Pew 1. Parents of the bride

Pew 2.

Pew 3.

Pew 4.

Pew 5.

Pew 6.

Groom's guests seated in reserved pews
Pew 1. Parents of the groom

Pew 2.

Pew 3.

Pew 4.

Pew 5.

Pew 6.

Special Notes

Head usher:
Usher to escort mother of the bride:
Usher to escort grandmother of the bride:
Usher to escort mother of the groom:
Usher to escort grandmother of the groom:

If the parents of the bride are divorced, where will mother (and step-father) sit?
Father and stepmother?
If the parents of the groom are divorced where will mother (and stepfather) sit?
Father and stepmother?

If the parents of either the bride or groom are divorced and the parents of the other are married you might consider this arrangement for the recessional: have the father of the bride escort the mother of the groom, and the father of the groom escort the mother of the bride. Of course this would not be practical if there were stepparents present and your own particular circumstances will dictate the proper solution for your wedding.

Notes on other special situations
(For example, if father of the bride is dead, who will escort her down the aisle? Where will he sit?, etc.)

$\mathcal{Y}$ou may choose to make your wedding ceremony extra special by including a favorite passage or poem to be read during service or even by writing your own vows. Jot down your thoughts here and be sure to discuss these with your clergyman.

_____

_____

_____

_____

_____

_____

_____

_____

Guests' responses (to be printed and passed out as guests enter church)

_____

_____

_____

_____

_____

_____

_____

_____

The Reception

Use this page to keep track of the arrangements made with your caterer. Be sure to transfer the name and address of your caterer to page 8.

Name:

Address:

Telephone:

Estimate:

    Price per guest ....$

    Gratuities...$

    Extras.. $

    Total price .... $

Number of waiters or waitresses:

Tables rented (number and price if not from caterer)

Tent, awning, etc. (size and price if not from caterer)

Number of guests:

    Number and shape of tables:

    Number of chairs at tables:

        Where rented (if not from caterer):

        Price:

Notes

_____

_____

_____

_____

_____

_____

_____

_____

Menu

> Hors d'oeuvres:
> Main course (if seated):
> Salad:
> Dessert:
> Sandwiches:
> Buffet dishes:
> Beverages:

Wedding Cake

> Where ordered:
> Name of salesperson:
> Description:
> Price:
> Time of delivery:
> Table for cake:
> Serving implements:

If you plan on a cocktail hour, list here the refreshments that will be offered during it:

Groom's Cake

Fruit cake cut in tiny squares and packaged in white boxes or paper, to be taken home by your guests for good luck. Very expensive if ordered from a bakery or caterer, but a friend might bake the cake and package it as a wedding gift.

Provided by: Price:

Receiving Line

Whether you want the attendants in the receiving line or not is entirely up to the two of you. Personally, I feel that it makes the line unnecessarily long. But this is something you two should decide together.

Order of line
    Mother of the bride
    (Father of the bride, optional)
    Mother of the groom
    (Father of the groom, optional)
    Bride
    Groom
    Maid of honor
    Bridesmaid
    Bridesmaid
    Bridesmaid
    Bridesmaid
    Bridesmaid

Guest Register

If you wish to have a guest register, you should select several friends to tend it and see that everyone who enters signs it. These friends, as well as special friends who may be asked to help serve punch, or cut and serve cake, are often known as "hostesses" or in some parts of the south "the house party." Make a list of these friends and try to arrange a schedule that divides the time each serves equally.

Hostesses

_____   _____

_____   _____

_____   _____

Bridal Table (if seated reception)

In addition to the bridal party, spouses and fiancés of the attendants should be seated at the bridal table. If you'll be using placecards, obtain them ahead of time, inscribe them and set them at their proper places.

_____	_____
_____	_____
_____	_____
_____	_____
_____	_____
_____	_____
_____	_____
_____	_____

Parents' Table

Parents of the bride
Parents of the groom
Grandparents
Godparents
Clergyman and spouse

If either set of parents is divorced, separate parents' tables should be set up so that the divorced pair need not sit together but each may sit apart with their own family or friends if that is preferred.

Photographs

Give the photographer a list of people you want included in formal photographs taken of bridal party at start of reception.

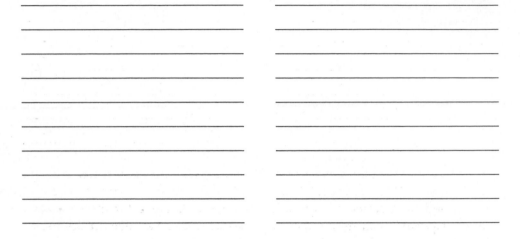

List of relatives and friends you want to be sure appear in candid photographs. Make a copy of this list and ask a close friend to point out these people to the photographer.

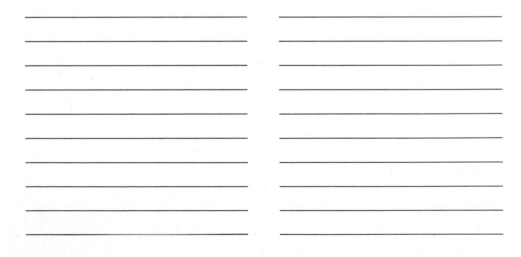

Musical Selections for Reception

Whether you have a strolling guitarist, a ten-piece orchestra, or music on a stereo tape deck, you will want certain personal favorites played. List them here as you think of them.

_____   _____

_____   _____

_____   _____

_____   _____

_____   _____

_____   _____

Go over your selections with your musicians, and ask a close friend to see that they have a list of them when the reception starts. If your music will be provided by a stereo or tape deck, arrange *in advance* for the selections you want played. You might also ask a friend to keep an eye on the music to see that continual music is played, if that's what you wish.

Bridal Registry and Your Pattern Selection

Many of your relatives and friends will want to know what you would like as a gift. The best way to help them choose, and to assure yourself that you will receive gifts that you want and need, is to register your choices at those stores in your community that have "bridal registries." When you list your choices in the stores try to select open patterns of china and crystal, patterns that will be available in the future if you wish to add to what you receive now. When you register, be sure to pick items in various price ranges to accommodate the budgets of all of your friends.

Some people object to the bridal registry as being too impersonal and commercial but I personally think it is an invaluable help to both bride and donor.

Pattern Selections

Fine china: _____

Stoneware, pottery, casual dinnerware: _____

Crystal: _____

Silverware: _____

Stainless: _____

Stores Where Gifts Are Registered

Name: _____

Address: _____   Telephone: _____

Registrar: _____

Name: _____

Address: _____   Telephone: _____

Registrar: _____

Name: _____

Address: _____   Telephone: _____

Registrar: _____

Name: _____

Address: _____   Telephone: _____

Registrar: _____

Gifts

Gift List

In order to keep your gifts organized, to know who gave what and where it came from in case of exchanges, and whether or not a thank-you has been sent, it is essential to keep an orderly gift list. You can get sheets of numbered stickers (or plain ones on which you can write a number) and affix one sticker in the correct column here and one with a corresponding number on the bottom of the gift. If you do this faithfully as the gifts arrive, there will be no possibility of confusion.

Gift No.	Description	Donor	Where Purchased	Date Rec'd	Thank You
0	Wooden salad bowl	Mr. & Mrs. Wm. Tell	Bloomingdale's	8/16	✔

Gift No.	Description	Donor	Where Purchased	Date Rec'd	Thank You

Gift No.	Description	Donor	Where Purchased	Date Rec'd	Thank You

Gift No.	Description	Donor	Where Purchased	Date Rec'd	Thank You

Gift No.	Description	Donor	Where Purchased	Date Rec'd	Thank You

Gift No.	Description	Donor	Where Purchased	Date Rec'd	Thank You

Gift No.	Description	Donor	Where Purchased	Date Rec'd	Thank You

Gift No.	Description	Donor	Where Purchased	Date Rec'd	Thank You

Gift No.	Description	Donor	Where Purchased	Date Rec'd	Thank You

Gift No.	Description	Donor	Where Purchased	Date Rec'd	Thank You

Exchanges and Replacements

Problems sometimes arise when gifts are delivered. Keep notes on exchanges, breakage, duplicate gifts you plan to exchange.

Exchanges
   Item exchanged:
   Replacement chosen: Donor:
   Store:

   Item exchanged:
   Replacement chosen: Donor:
   Store:

   Item exchanged:
   Replacement chosen: Donor:
   Store:

Breakage
   Item broken:
   Store where purchased: Donor:

   Item broken:
   Store where purchased: Donor:

Duplicates and Other Problems:

Gifts for Attendants

While the two of you have been the recipients of many lovely gifts you should attempt to bestow upon those family and friends who served in your bridal party a gift that expresses your true feelings toward them as well as your gratitude.

Maid of honor's gift:
  Store: Salesperson:
  Date ordered: Delivery date: Price:

Matron of honor's gift:
  Store: Salesperson:
  Date ordered: Delivery date: Price:

Bridesmaids' gifts:
  Store: Salesperson:
  Date ordered: Delivery date: Price:

Flower girl's gift:
  Store: Salesperson:
  Date ordered: Delivery date: Price:

Best man's gift:
  Store: Salesperson:
  Date ordered: Delivery date: Price:

Ushers' gifts:
  Store: Salesperson:
  Date ordered: Delivery date: Price:

Ring Bearer's gift:
  Store: Salesperson:
  Date ordered: Delivery date: Price:

The Newspaper Announcement

If you want your wedding to be announced in the newspapers, you will be expected to provide the newspaper with the necessary information, and also a photograph, if you wish. Large city newspapers have their own forms which they will send you at your request. Smaller newspapers will want your notice sent to them at least ten days or two weeks in advance and the sooner you do so, the more certain you can be that your announcement will appear. Newspapers only print as many announcements as space permits. They may rework your wording or may eliminate some of the information you send. Send the information to the Society Editor—if there is none it will be forwarded to the correct department. Make sure to include a release date and also a phone number where either of you can be reached in case the newspaper seeks to verify any information.

Newspaper announcement will be sent to:

Name of newspaper:
Address:

Name of newspaper:
Address:

Name of newspaper:
Address:

It is also courteous to ask the mother of the groom whether she would like the announcement sent to her local papers. Or, she may send the announcement in herself if she has personal contacts at the newspaper.

Before writing your own wedding announcement, read those in your local paper. Select the wording you like best, and if you are lucky, yours will be printed in just that way.

Information That Should be Included in the Announcement

Bride's full name
Bride's parents' name and address
Bride's parents' occupations
Bride's maternal and paternal grandparents
Bride's school and college
Bride's occupation
Groom's full name and address
Groom's parents' name and address
Groom's parents' occupations
Groom's maternal and paternal grandparents
Groom's school and college
Groom's occupation

Date of wedding
Location of wedding and reception
Names of bride's attendants (relationship to bride or groom)
Names of groom's attendants (relationship to bride or groom)
Description of bridal gown
Description of attendants' costumes
Name of minister
Name of soloist (if any)
Where couple will honeymoon
Where couple will reside after wedding

Use this space to plan the wording of the announcement if your newspaper does not send you a form to fill out.